Just As

Just As

POEMS

by

Julius Jortner

Painting on cover is
"Heart's Beat"
by Thomas Goodwin
(Acrylic on canvas, 1998, 24"x36")
used with his permission

ISBN: 978-1505276701
Library of Congress Control Number: 2015902622

Made in the United States of America
by
CreateSpace Independent Publishing Platform
North Charleston, SC

This book is dedicated to the memory of my parents:

Michał Jortner
(1895-1959)

and

Maria Jortner (née Spielvogel)
(1901-1972)

"We write to create ourselves, to discover, moment to moment to moment, who we are and who we are becoming."

--Paulann Petersen

Contents

BLANK PAGE

RANDOM THOUGHTS

REMNANTS (early poems 1974-2004)

ENCOUNTERS

ON THE ROAD HOME

HOLLYWOOD DREAMS

AWARE

EVENING FLIGHT

DAILY RITUAL

RAIN

ONLY ME

UNLEASHED

IN THE CLEAR

JUST AS

***

BLANK PAGE

BLANK PAGE

An ache
precedes this

a yearning
to express

to push out
something live

something firm
yet subtle

a cry of its own
its beauty in its truth

WHEN I WRITE

usually I've chosen a direction to go
not that I keep to it
but the first decision has been made

like kicking off onto a bicycle
mounting while it begins its journey, holding on
to the handlebars, adjusting direction,
finding the path to be taken

hoping to arrive
where meaning makes itself known
a place hospitable to a picnic of tangerine,
an embrace, a nap, and a dream

WHAT IT MEANS

"What's my number?
I wonder how your engine feels"
            -    Paul Simon, *Baby Driver*

Why give my poems to public scenes
(ink of magazines on pages white
or phosphors on a screen of light)
to reveal myself to you?

Will all be read by neighbors
down the street
or in cities on the map
or heard by those in chairs
up the stairs in Newport by the beach?

My eyes mist – I almost weep
to hope my thoughts arrive
in the cosy folds of your frontal lobes
in your secret sleep.

I show you my words
because I want to know
how your engine feels -
especially if you're a woman
oh my oh yes
but even if a man or boy or girl -
if you'll tell me I exist
and what it means.

WHY WRITE?

I want to find my need
to blind my dread
and show to myself
(and to the you I imagine)
who is to blame
how did it happen
what brings us here
burdened by these trunks of sorrow?

AMBIGUITIES

for David

I sometimes inject them
or don't remove them,
to give you a choice... but
you might see meanings I did not know
as you read a poem richer than I'd written.

Years from now I too might read it and say,
"How complex and clever!" or, more likely,
"Did I really write this and what does it mean?"

At a recent open mic, I read a poem
I'd made to convey quotidian moods
and random thoughts.
David offered "That's a love poem!"
I said, "That is not what I meant at all."

"And that," he answered, "is the power of poetry."

LATE AMBITIONS

When I was young
the path was high
and the peaks nearby
were high too.

As I age
the path declines
but at each stage
are peaks to climb.

Some of these
though not so high
as some of yore
are higher than any
I'd attained before.

Diminished strength
need not impede –
I'll choose my goals
plot my steps -
wit and art
shall be my steeds.

While nothing long
defers Time's end -
while I'm able
I'll ascend.

THEORETICAL QUESTIONS FOR AMATEUR POETS

Some say poems come mainly in unhappiness.

Does anything new come from contentment?
Does contentment ever demand work
at the cost of interrupting itself?
Questions irrelevant for a Stafford
who rose before dawn each day
to write a poem before he did else.

Easy to sit down to write
if an urge happens.
If no urge, habit may help.

First comes the writing.
Then, if I am a poet, comes a poem.
If I am not a poet, at least I am a writer.
Even only a writer might write a poem on occasion.

Perhaps poems do come from those who seldom write.
We do not know from reading or hearing a poem
how much writing made it.

SOMETIMES WAITING IS THE PRIZE

I saw the stocky man standing
on the roadside river bank
his pole steady in hand
his line in the water waiting.

In the long seconds it took
to pass him then lose him
from the rearview mirror
he seemed to not move.

My father was a city man
an engineer
who taught me constellations
who told of walking country woods
inhaling fresh air on mountain paths
crossing streams from rock to rock
looking at stars in country dark
who never mentioned fishing.

I too became an engineer
before doing this:

Paper pad resting on thighs
I sit still with pen tip steady
against the page
waiting for a fresh word to rise
to pen baited with curiosity and thirst
my mind (I imagine) like the fisherman's
at peace in calm anticipation.

Both of us wait to catch a prize
to complete a meal or a poem
a catch the stillness of this moment
makes possible but is sufficient without.

RANDOM THOUGHTS

TAUGHT BY SALT

She had flown into the city that morning.
We drove to my small coastal town, unpacked,
and now walk to the high dune, high enough
it obscures the sea. We are glad to stretch.
As we climb, the horizon lifts into view - bang!
a fat wind buffets our ears, fills our coats
and embraces our ribs. We see wild foam
and bleached logs decorate the hard sands
below, where my black dog runs, ears aflap.
The big rock is dark against the sky to the right.
Clouds drift gray-white over the aquamarine.
Mad squawks of gulls slice through the roar of surf.
   I turn to her. There are tears on her cheeks!
   Astonished, I don't cry then - I have since.

RANDOM THOUGHTS

Placing one vegetable then another
in the pot of boiling water
makes soup

Onion ginger garlic
and potatoes in a pot -
hot water becomes soup

The richest soup starts
with just one vegetable
in the boiling water

Once more life rises
from a long night of warm sleep -
gently swelling cock

Craving warm applause
but ignored or scorned?
drink red wine
move on

Journals reject you?
lower your sights
post to Facebook
be happy to be liked

Drops drizzle windshield
wisps of mist float over hills
dreams hide in the distance

I am hoping
your mind receives my thought
though it's enough to write it

Charge ahead my friend
force a path with your brilliance –
I bob in your wake

MOOD

This change though spare
not tumultuous
still strips bare
our comfortable skin
scraping
us here and there
as we hurt
or lie inert
our nature changing
grain by grain
like a sand dune in
the not quite soft breeze
never quite the same again

THE ANCIENT DORYMAN

limps old knees bent
till in the dory standing
he rows over the white surf

IMAGININGS

as prelude to a nap
imaginings of blue tattoos
on plump brown skin
lead my dreams astray

NEW TRICKS

Age, heartless thief,
stole only the ambitions of youth.
Now, any new thing done,
keeps delight alive.

DIFFIDENCE

allows only the shallow probe
of chaste respect
leaves untouched the core
unexplored the unknown

ANONYMOUS ONLINE

Let pixels tell
All you want us to know about who –
Let pixels hide
Your universal private blue

WINTER MORNING IN THE CITY

silent white powder
soon streaked black wet grey and loud
by Manhattan's cars

THE LAUREL TREE

I wake alone
Leaves brush my window
Your warmth is gone
And waking is slow

Leaves brush my window
Light seeps onto the bed
And waking is slow
Nothing is said

Light seeps onto the bed
My sight floats free
Nothing is said
Just the rustling laurel tree

My sight floats free
Your warmth is gone
Just the rustling laurel tree
I wake alone

IT'S AS IF I NEED NOT EXIST

I smile through the day
gathering warmth from others
presenting to them a person
who does not exist.

A DREAM

I dreamt the little elevator
coffinlike crammed
three of us
the others men
naked sort of with stiffening penises
and one brushes his lips against mine
although it's clear they are a couple
I the stranger
a potential plaything.

I have no time for this -
nor inclination.

There is the question of insurance
and credit cards
a contract I'd signed.

I stay in a hotel
or is it an apartment... no,
it is on a metal table that I sleep.

The car needs fixing
so I control it remotely
to speed towards a plateau
a field of stones and grass
where I think to leave it for a while.

On impulse, I accelerate the empty car till
its speed equals my age at the moment
it reaches the ramp to the field.

The car is air-borne very high, flips several times,
and lands on wheels, bounces high, flips over,
lands again hard, parts scattering, bounces and lands,
such noise, landing finally a pancake
as might have fallen off a stack from a salvage truck.

Day breaks, other cars commute to work
ignoring my car's corpse. Children play in the field.

I'd committed to take delivery of newspapers.
The bundle tied with string arrives.
They don't yet know the car is destroyed
that I am useless to them.

NOCTURNE

A high California moon is waxing
Ripe mangoes peep lamplit from their tree
My mind opens wide to my memory of
Candle glow on your breasts over me

SUDDEN CLOSENESS

"After cataract surgery, you might get along
without glasses much of the time," said the eye doctor.

Without glasses, intimacy -
or so it's been
since I became a lover -
so now with cataracts gone
new eyes clear and sharp
I see you (whoever you are)
facing me as we talk
and I feel close to you
as if we lay together on a bed
nothing between you and me.

WASTING AWAY

wishing to become
if only we knew what
we wander half awake
among the desires of others
their detrita distracting as we float
through tangled tubes of trance
aiming for hazy hills distant
in the ivory mist

TOO LATE THIS DREAM

I dream of walking away
walking across the country
having given away possessions
obligations abandoned

walking into simplicity
taking time when and where
time happens
unencumbered

but when I walk the quarter mile
from house to post office and back
I get tired
my hips hurt

and I know walking away
may not happen
because I tire
and I want to lie down

easier to walk away in mind alone
without exposure or fatigue
       let this man's thoughts travel
       let his imagination see

AN AGING MAN'S HOUSE

"One aged man—one man—can't keep a house..."
Robert Frost, *An Old Man's Winter Night*

While it's true he weakens or forgets, it's not just that.

He'd rather gaze at the moon above the dark trees,
or sit in thought by the fire stove.
Write, perhaps.

What he ought, in the eyes of the young,
falls behind working out the puzzle of his life -
telling his story, tendering himself to a friend
more important than excavating rot.

His greatest wealth is time.

REMNANTS

early poems, 1974 - 2004

ARIZONA NIGHT

Sandwiched
Between high desert
And cloud feathered sky
We lay
Skinscapes open to warm breeze puffs
Ruffling armpits' hair.

Some stars
Startlingly sharp
Pale pinks and blues
Sent stips of pleasure
Into pupils already overwhelmed
By a haloed half moon.

Rain came.
Large wet kisses woke.
But it was over before we could flee.

The arid air
Sucked back the drops
Leaving us dry and cool
To watch the sun's rise.

FIRST DATE AT MARIO'S

Side by side
Just as we drove
And waited for a table
We sit at Mario's
Facing an elongated room
Of oddly arranged people.

Shoulder to shoulder
Our arms
Moving to move food
Separate us.

Eye-borne exclamations
Facial flicks
Instant intimations,
Unseen
Are they really there at all?

As I turn to catch a glance,
Spaghetti tails glide into the far corner
Of my mouth.
Oblique looks
Artificially skeptical
Accompany slanted questions
Deflected thoughts.

(Missing is the social savor
Of seeing your enjoyment mirror mine
With two eyes squarely eyeing two
As Italian morsels work their charm.)

Easy to look down on
The back of your hand
Structure of graceful bone and rings
Hoping for a glimpse
Of soft palm
Imagined warmth
Amorphous and accommodating
In its folds.

Conversation lapses.
Bursts of words
Traveling outward to the other wall
Don't bounce back.
Synchronous chewing spreads silence.

I am grateful for the wine
Dark red and oily smooth
It soothes and envelops
As we float forward
Side by side
Shoulder to shoulder
Towards an unknown destination.

REMNANTS

Recalcitrant residuals
Resisting resolution
Will you dissolve in Time,
Digester of dream and delusion?
Or will you bloom again
If some warm wind brings rain?

BLACK ON BLUE

Black dog paws and tail
Five quarter notes of night
Shake a hole
In the lace edge of the sea.

Black wing grazing pellucid swell,
A pelican on his shadow glides.
Two gulls follow flapping.

On the horizon
An island rips the sky
Leaving sharp edges.

DAYDREAM

In the shade I laze the day
Feeling warm air caress my thigh
Wishing life simpler than it is
Hoping for joy tomorrow.

LEGACY

The aging man asks,
Where are the young bloods?
I've been pushing these boulders
Making a clearing
For whom?

TECHNOLOGIST'S APOLOGY

If you asked us what are we working for
And by what rules do we guide ourselves
Could we answer?

We solve little problems here and there
For the personal Aha! of understanding
Hoping someone understands we understand
Although we know what we understand
Serves an artificial game –

Our understanding makes us capable
Of advising those who don't
Helps them accomplish ends
We would not choose.

They pay for this
And we live well.

PERSPECTIVE

Once I boasted (to a rich man)
"For me it's not the money
That rewards.
It is the work itself.
I will never retire."

Today I tire
And wish I were rich.

COMPLAINT

How can I dance carrying this load?

Is the load imaginary?
Can I put it down to rest?
Must I drop it?
Can it get smaller?

They say a well-posed question
Points to, Implies, Contains
Its own answer.

The problem is to find that question.

A locked trunk,
       With the key inside

HAVING STUMBLED

Having stumbled
He struggles to rise.

What might have been
Had he not fallen
We shall never know.

   .

DEADLINES

To my wife, "Saturday we will travel
To show your tender grandsons the big city
To fertilize their minds."

To my client, "This weekend before I leave
You will have my report
Telling your people all they need
About that obscure topic
You asked me to probe."

To those who say, "Promise
Only what you can deliver."
I say, "Overcommitment is a sign
Of a genial and optimistic nature."

Frightened by the disappearing week,
I slept.

Saturday, rolling from the station on the train,
I've let slip one promise to keep the other
Exposed, again, a liar.

Oh well.

Had I died on Friday
Breaking both promises
Would they think better of me?

AT THE MALL

1. Young Couple

Her chin on his shoulder
Her hands in his pockets
She waddles behind him giggling
As they approach the gift shop.

2. On Lunch Break

Three guys
Serious with ties
And dark-rimmed glasses
Walking fast.

Six hands in pockets
Weaving bodies, bobbing heads
Trailing sheets of words
Through which others pass.

3. Married

In matching tee shirts
Shoulder to shoulder
Eyes level and fearless
They glide.

Each right hand holds one
Of the steaming white cups
That pull them along.

4. Dangerous Pet

Wrist attached to her wrist
With red springy phonecord,
The boy, four and bored,
Sits with his mother.
She gathers up her packages.
He rises and takes
A waiting position
Six feet away.

The running teenager clears
The taut red line
By two inches.

.

OVERCOME

What if all came easy
A ripe mango
Already peeled and diced
No strings?

I would be overcome
By insomnia or sleep.

To overcome
To feel alive
Use skill and wit
Solve the problem
Escape the deep
Throw the frisbee
Watch it fly
No strings.

THE GREEN MOHAVE

The speeding shadow of our sleeper
Draws on rain bright sands
Memories of our destination
Where we no longer live

LIMP APOLOGY

When I applied my lips to yours
Stretching skin
Making one dark space within
A continuum from end to end,

And thoughts of
      Hands, mouths, pulling, sucking, patting,
      Children,
      Lover,
      Father,
      Caring and demanding,
      Touching your bones and skin, your
      Heart and brain,
Squeezed from the caverns of my head and chest
Out my mouth into ours,

There seemed no need to press
Bulb-tipped penis
Against that ancient mossy landscape
Five thousand miles away down there.

But, oh, sweet love
It would have been nice
To give and take both ends like that
Had I been able to.

SOARING

Soaring might be falling.

Do I know the difference?

Help me!

One can fall a long time and think one is flying
given the gift of a high starting point.

The arc of one's life becomes apparent
only in retrospect.

Given much...

Squandered...

Splat!

Rise again.

ENCOUNTERS

WOMEN AT THE TAVERN

1. Loneliness

I kissed her
She kissed me back
A stranger
Tentatively
Wondering to what end
This contact will lead.

She wants to introduce me
To her mother. Yet
I kissed her and she kissed me.

But she was drunk, she said.
And I was tentative, knowing
The twenty years between us
Might mean
I'll kiss her mother too.

2. One dance

She follows my moves
Before I make them
Keeping close
Leg along leg
Chest to chest
Hand solid in hand.

Once before
I felt unity like this.
It endured till
Death did us part.

Tonight I'm held
By a careless girl
For this dance only.

3. Teased

She smiled to see me
Bought me a glass of wine
Said she'd like to be
My friend – did I understand
We were to be just friends –
Did I see how much she wanted
To be friends first?

She embraced me
As she rose to leave
Kissed me full on the mouth –
A look in the eyes -
Wants me over for dinner
Hopes I'm no vegan.

When I moved to kiss her
She turned her cheek to my lips.

4. Belief

Her widely placed fair-lashed eyes
Sometimes blue sometimes green
Look at me as her small mouth smiles
Yummm! she murmurs and
Although I think she's said this before
To others... I believe her.

ENCOUNTERS

1. *Grandma*

She is trim
about my age
and working
at the fast food place.

"This is for you, grandma,"
said the young supervisor -
a carton of napkins
to be placed on the tables.

The woman looks at me
and shrugs a smile,
as if to say,
"The young ones don't know, do they?"

Or, perhaps, he really is her grandson.
Small town.

2. *Envy*

White beard framing a lined face
the slender beef-jerky of a man
approaches
his tee-shirt loose in
jeans hanging from wide suspenders.

I want his body
wishing too to have that space
between belly and clothes -
perhaps it's not too late
to regiment my life
to make my pillowed self
fit to please my eye.

3. Beauty

Pale blue eyes
magnified by the lenses
on her thinning face
a death's head smile
of bright false teeth.

Do her eyes shift back and forth
or does her head tremble around them?

The easy sureness of youth is gone.

Yet, I see the tall full-lipped blonde
she must have been back then
coveted by her husband's friends
and by strangers
arousing desire
wherever she went.

4. Women's Liberation

Four white-haired women
out for the evening
share a booth at the Thai restaurant
their faces calmer
their demeanor more relaxed
than when their husbands were alive.

In their seventies, I'd guess,
and healthy -
they expect years
of freedom ahead.

5. Pretense

The woman walking by
is acknowledged only
by my stillness
as I gaze down the walkway
and do not turn my head
while she passes.

6. Progress

He walks in
with the other woman
we've heard of -
her face familiar -
a younger healthier version
of his wife.

7. Woman on Bar Stool

Regal nose, black-rim glasses,
red lips sharply defined -
the face, severe with black coiff,
is intimidating and strange
but its expressions are familiar.
So too is the language of the body
her plump thigh pressed
against his, her rounded
shoulder nesting in his armpit.
So familiar that I imagine feeling
the warmth between them.
I know this woman is a woman
now, whatever she may have seemed
in the office an hour or so ago.

8. Feck

The woman's tee said "Feck You!"
but she smiled at me as she passed.

When did I begin to feel feckless
unable to focus and finish
anything
except these poems
which come and accumulate
and get revised?

What would a woman want with me?
someone with
no money no prospects?
perhaps a seductive manner, but
what really to offer but
the momentary warmth
of a needy kiss?

I should get a tee shirt
"Wants feck".

I'M NOT A RABBI

"Hello, Rabbi"
said the tall young man
as he passed behind me
an evening ago
in this coastal Oregon town.

I don't know him
beyond sightings
in street and tavern
and I wonder and fear
the possibilities.

Is "Hey Jew" what he meant?

Does he suspect
I like to think of
a local grandmother
a Christian woman?

I wonder and fear
the possibilities
of pain induced
along the nerves of pleasure.

Or perhaps he respects me?
My age?

Perhaps he knows rabbi means teacher.

But I'm not a teacher either.

REFUGEES

A big dusty raccoon
patters across my wood deck at noon
like a rumpled old man woken from a nap
displaced from a forest home somewhere
drawn by need to this coastal village
on this first sunny day in May.

Next day
there are two raccoons
walking down my hill's dirt drive
one after the other
swaying from side to side
refugees from a home somewhere.

They look brittle and unhappy.
Why are they about at noon?

What do they eat?
Has there been a recession
in their economy too?
Are they neighbors now
not tourists or visiting friends?

They ignore me watching them.
They belong here, they say, even as they
seem just passing through.
It's their land too.

How many tomorrow?

ON THE ROAD HOME

HEADING HOME IN WINTER

shadows of sparse pines
crossing the road
might remind a poet
of the coming long night
but the driver
speeding west at noon
sees equal bars of dark and light
like cattle guards of only paint
and crosses smoothly
to the sunlit plain beyond

ALONG THE INTERSTATE

Smell of orange blossoms.
Here, gone.

Vistas pass by
many worth remembering wild
some asking for capture
in a rectangular frame.

Everywhere I look, almost,
there are such pictures to be had.

(Everywhere I look, in my mind,
there is a woman...)

Too many to stop for.

Used to be
this very road seemed boring...
(older women too)

Now
views of the vast flat land
ringed by brown hills
sometimes golden
(clouds and their shadows
pale colors
dark trees scattered
complex subtle)
fascinate
and older women
now my age
(or younger)
complex subtle
arouse life in me.

ON THE ROAD HOME

We roll off the driveway
crackling leaves under my red car.

The road opens.
Light rain falls from the sheet of gray cloud.
A strip of buttery light promises clear sky.
We speed for that horizon.

What are we leaving behind?
What waits ahead?
Who are we?

My hand rests on your thigh
as I drive. Sometimes
your hand rests on mine.
We talk.
We allow ourselves to think.
We anticipate.

There will be nights in motels
our bodies fitting tightly .

Are we driving to your home? mine?

We've done this before
but not with each other.
We know how to be
on journeys like this.
We like not being alone.

ON THE EDGE

As my mind travels apart
tires drift from the sodden road
to its grassy edge
and the car slides
a sidewise glide.

My feet leave the pedals.
Hands hold steady the wheel
during this liberation from control.
A grassy arc brings us back
to the appointed path.

Sixty feet down
the creek plays with broken trees.

DOWN THE ROAD NEAR COALINGA

Two dogs asleep in the back seat
the woman next to me strokes my hand
to music from the radio on a sunlit interstate
as we head for a leafy walk and
lunch at a café or picnic on a slope
miles beyond this stench of cattle
hundreds corralled on dark acres
of trampled earth unspecked by any green
standing still and silent
(are they ill from the fattening grain
dreaming grass fields and fresh breeze?)
being finished into marbled meat
for neon-lit steakhouses and food for dogs.

HOLLYWOOD DREAMS

MEMORIES AT STARBUCKS IN HOLLYWOOD

1. Bill

He is seventy-seven, he says,
gray beard long unkempt,
dark glasses hiding his eyes
his upper denture dancing on its own
as he speaks, dressed in a neatly pressed
starched khaki shirt over baggy plaid slacks.
"My name is Bill," he says
as I sit across the little table outside.

He is glad his check is coming
tomorrow, the first of May.
The government has not paid him for months.
When was the last time? He thinks a while,
before saying "April eleventh".
This year?
"Yes."

He is a playwright he says and recently realized
all 23 of his plays have the same story.

What is that story?
Doesn't matter – they're just comedies –
nothing but dialog back and forth.

The first was a hit.
He tells me its name
(and indeed when I google later
there it is - attributed to a William ---)
he doesn't recall the others
hasn't written for a while

and the first, it was big
in the sixties, he thinks it was,
made it from LA to NewYork.

They all just came to him
voices and all he had to do
is write them down
but now? his memory is going
and he has not written.

Are the voices silent? or
can he simply not write them down any more?
He doesn't answer.

2. The Man in the Green Cap

The fair-skinned man with gray curls and blue eyes, clean-
shaven, dressed well, perhaps in his seventies, asks me
how's life and, for some reason, I find myself telling him
that I have been writing some poetry. He says he is a
writer, but not of poetry. He has written a couple of
poems, one of which he always carries with him in his shirt
pocket. But not today. It's on his dresser, that piece of
folded paper. He would recite it for me, but says he has
difficulty remembering things. Especially words. But
they'll come, if he relaxes.

He remembers giving his sister, younger than he, a present
when she was a girl. That's what the poem is about. Then,
of a sudden, out his mouth comes the poem, a lovely simple
set of lines evoking a young girl's delight. He also had
written another poem, but ...

He wears a baseball cap, green, with two embroidered
yellow lines: "UCLA" over "KV5". I ask about UCLA, saying

I went to school there. The KV stands for Valley of the Kings, he says. Doesn't remember what the 5 means... it'll come to him. This Valley was a special place. Very few people know of it. He tells me of a man, very famous, I'd know this man, the name will come to him... who once saw him in the cap and asked, "Where did you get that? Do you know what it means?" When he told the man about the Valley of the Kings, the man invited him to a mansion in Beverly Hills and they talked a long time. And UCLA? He takes off the cap and looks at it. Oh, I have lots of these... only some have UCLA on them, don't recall why.

He has not seen his sister for a couple of years. Last time he phoned, in December, they refused to talk to him.

He used to be in touch with his sisters, especially at Christmas he'd send cards to his nieces and nephews. Not lately. He has difficulty writing, can't remember words, doesn't want to expose himself as lacking, thinks his silence has offended them, his younger sisters, who don't know how in need he is.

He has been working on a movie script and tells me the story. He keeps it in his mind. The story is of a prostitute (to be played by Madonna), who leaves (retires from) the brothel in the States to travel to Italy to meet a powerful man (known as "El Duce") because she has worshipped his power from afar. Soon after landing, she meets a pleasant fellow at the airport. He befriends her and helps her find her way. There are scenes of them riding through Rome on his motor scooter. She learns El Duce is scheduled to attend a conference of film directors. She plies her trade among the directors, despite the apparent fact her new friend has fallen in love with her, hoping to meet this El Duce. Eventually, word spreads. El Duce hears of her and sends his car. When she arrives at his mansion, she is ushered into a room where a man sits with his back to the door. He turns and, ohmygosh, it's her friend from the airport! El Duce had to let her find her own way to him. Did I see it coming? he asks me. His sisters are old-fashioned, wouldn't appreciate a story like that. He has written eighteen scripts, all residing in his mind, none on paper. But... he stumbles for words, which will come soon if he relaxes.

HOLLYWOOD DREAMS

1.

Sitting outside the cafe
the woman
solid and fifty
takes off her shoes
and carefully places
her clean white-stockinged feet
on the new paper towel
she'd spread on the walkway.

She adjusts her feet
to be parallel to the
towel's edges.
When she turns her head my way
I see scabby wounds on her nose and lip.
Her eyes don't see me.

She turns back to her feet
and speaks softly

"Worthless!"

 "Ugly!"

 "Fat!"

 pauses and nods her head

"That may be true,
 but O God,
 you think you're so clever
 to torture somebody so."

2.

The tall thirtyish man stood
by the entrance to the drugstore.
He wore unwrinkled clothes
a clean black overjacket
a plaid woolly scarf
sunglasses
denim slacks
clean sneakers.

"Can you spare some change?" he asked.

I looked at him, "Are you living on the street?"

"Yes."

We talked a bit, about keeping warm,
having a pot to piss in
(he mentioned Denny's and Jack in the Box),
about the freedom...

Then I said,

"Please feel free to not answer,
 but how is it for human companionship?"

Without hesitation, he answered,

"You have to be prepared to be lonely."

3.

Emerging from the bar
across the street
the young man hangs his head
holding a cell phone to his ear.

Suddenly
I hear him

"You're lying!"

His head is up.
He is shouting

"You're lying!"

He leans against the building
hangs his head
and listens.

OUTSIDE THE KARMA COFFEEHOUSE

The public face is ready to be donned
if asked, "How are you?
How are things going?"
The preferred answer
"Okay, I guess, can't complain"
must come with no belying hesitation...
despite my longing to be true
to be seen
to make contact...

But no one is asking.
They pass by one by one
two by two or three.

I see the couples on this Sunday morning
...the first date - walking apart but in touch
...the lovers hip to hip
...the long married, separate,
   looking around glum to see what they're missing
...the long married, together, talking, shoulders touching
...the lovers hand in hand
...the fathers with children
...the girl with hers on her hip.

A woman approaches alone
talking on a cell phone
and enters the coffeehouse.

Another woman alone
smiles at my dog
and passes unwavering.

All have some purpose.

I am alone
and have no purpose
but to write this.

WALK DOWN VINE STREET

Woman on electric cart asleep
in middle of sidewalk
cheek against handlebar
mouth ajar with unconscious teeth.

Pigeon standing at wall
uneasy eyes
shifting from one leg to the other
unable to fly.

A crowd gathered outside
coffee shop after AA meeting
loudly chattering
unintimate contact
unwilling to go home.

Damaged creatures
all capable of pleasure
given food
water to drink
water to wash
and love
a warm place to sleep.

Did I say given? Do I mean charity?

Did I say love? Do I mean caresses?

And is that all that is needed?

The thin dark man talks to himself
meeting no one's eye,

Kill the fuckers!
Cocksuckers!
Sonsabitches!
Shitters all.

I WALK THE STREETS, OPEN

I walk the streets, open to contact. I think of sex. But not sex. Touch. Breasts against my chest. Hands on my skin. I crave. I am hollow for lack of. I ache with longing. I want to lie against a woman. Who? Does it matter? I think of many. I long for contact. Not with the young. Who are they? Might as well have a rubber doll. Too perfect. No. I long for contact with a mature woman, worn, with used breasts and knowing hands, and an open heart. But not just one. No, no particular one. Not one. But many. Or none. Will it be none? I think of B-, who is married and caring for a dying husband. I think of K-, who is unmarried but on the other coast, much younger than I and perhaps promiscuous. I think of V-, who lives with a woman to whom she is devoted, but whose chaste kiss on my lips raised my hopes. I think of Z-, who is strong and tan and wrinkled, with steel-gray hair tied in a top knot, who may or may not be single, who may or may not be lesbian, who may or may not be nuts, but who has broad shoulders and heavy breasts and is quick to talk, who laughs and has an apartment overlooking the ocean, which she told me about and offered me a seat on her balcony. I think of T-, whose mother just died, who is awkward and unhappy, wasting away from overwhelming stress, perhaps a brain disease, married to an idiot. I think of another T-, whose mother also just died, who is married to an admirable guy in a wheelchair, an enormous woman whose hug enveloped me and felt so good. I think of M-, so tall and thin, witty and acerbic, living unhappily with her estranged but needy husband in one apartment. I think of D-, recently retired career woman living alone in a nearby town, but I don't know her and I don't know if I like her, though she looked awfully good to me the other day with small breasts moving under a fine salmon-colored sweater. And I think of my C-, who died. She is gone, and here are all these others, none of whom are mine, none of whom do I want to be mine. But, oh, I so wish I could touch them, one or all, and be touched, embrace and be embraced, sleep with, nuzzle with, feel. So, I am open to contact, and find almost everybody responds to me, will talk to me and listen to what I say. I am open, and try to tell the truth. I don't know if body touches will follow someday, but I have hopes - or daydreams, rather. I don't know what I hope for. I need. I crave. I am hollow with longing. I walk the streets, looking at women.

AWARE

PERSONAL AD

I seek a woman
clean and understanding
of this aging man,
not a woman waiting
to be overcome
by prowess or strength,
penetrated roughly with gusto
by a young bull.
I need one who needs caresses
likes to give them
who takes the lead herself at times.
A woman of an age
with scars to prove it
who has lived enough
to have something to say
yet remains curious
who would enjoy slow touch
and soft embrace
be willing to talk
before and during
the dance of senses and mind
who is as hungry as I
who would like to kiss and stroke
and press against me
who would laugh at my jokes
and my pretensions
who speaks what she sees and knows
who is willing to be admired
by me.

If you think you'd want
to spend time with the man
who writes this, please respond
in the way only you would know.

IS SHE FLIRTING?

above the half smile of her comely mouth
she looks at me, intimate and challenging,
as we stand outside the meeting room
while shadows of her smooth cleavage
leap past the vee-open blouse.

I find it easy to smile back
to meet the challenge
to meet her gaze and talk
after acknowledging her breasts
with a slow tour of my eye.

GIFTS FROM WOMEN

of course the first to give was my mother
but I talk of lesser gifts

warm socks
a pullover sweater
there is the lovely corkscrew
its curves fitting well in the palm
two tee shirts
a sky-blue silk shirt
the hairbrush of natural bristle
a polished wood bellows for the firestove
a book inscribed
a sturdy leather belt

each of these
valued less at the time
than warmth of arms and lips
when used reminds of the giver
who thus gives pleasure still

AWARE

of the open smiles
of the women
as we pass each other
in the street
at the factory
or engage gazes
at a restaurant
or on the bus

I imagine
legs open for
touch
kiss
the belly waiting for
caress
the waist
with little folds
of flesh
skin smooth
waiting to be held.

I wonder
do they smile
to see me
as old and safe
beyond it all
or because they see me
as old and knowing
aware and
available?

I see each body
attached to that smile
the pendant breasts
the moist armpits
the pubic hair
the kissing thighs
the skin
the skin
the skin
the warmth
the hot warmth
of secret places
while looking
in her eyes.

ABOUT GIVING UP SEX

Prince Gautama became aware
of earthly suffering
and changed his life
to maintain that awareness
of the pain of others
and his own.

The awareness was almost enough.
He also gave up royal luxury
and, still young, gave up
the pleasures of the flesh,
to become the buddha.

I am not young, but
cannot willingly abandon
some of those pleasures.

As an old man, Gandhi, the Mahatma,
slept naked next to the warm skins
of young women.
Some think it was hypocritical of him
to advocate abstinence
while allowing himself such contact.
He was testing himself, he said, to
prove himself free of carnal desire.

Well... okay, just as sex and love are not the same,
touching and sex are not the same... but
would he have dared test himself
in the hot embrace of an equal,
a mature woman with knowing hands,
perhaps even his wife?

What is it about sex
that must be avoided
if one is to be enlightened?

When I walk alone
I can feel
the sorrow
and the peace
of the world around.

If I walk with you
hand in hand
my friend, my lover,
I feel our bond.

My mate and I
    ... on our skins
    we write
    the stories of our being
    feeling
    what we make each other feel
    a prayer made by two

Any mammal I've known
will sleep in contact
with another warm beast
if available and willing.

I think of my body warm
entwined with a woman....

Will pleasure make us
crave ever more?
give up honor for it?
sacrifice the welfare of others for it?
become buried in it? enslave us?

It is said pain and pleasure
are two sides of a coin.
Can't have one without the other.
Will giving up pleasure avoid pain?
There is this difference...
We can and often do deliberately
cause pain to other creatures.
We cannot ensure its absence for ourselves.
Not even giving up pleasure will do that.

SLEEPING WITH A FRIEND

*"And the lion shall lie down with the calf,
 but the calf won't get much sleep."*
                          -    Woody Allen

When in your flannel pajamas
a red plaid of warmth
you lay down by me on the bed
I wanted to open the buttons
kiss your red nipple and lick your red lips.

But I held back.

So we slept there together
touching shoulders and thighs
feeling friendship in comfort and heat.

Neither of us got much rest.

CAUTION

In this small town
a blinking red light
asks you to not go
before stopping.

In this small town
a woman is noticed
her movements and
involvements known
and a man's appearances
with one and then another
tracked
by sightings
of couples
and recognition of cars
parked over night.

So it is simpler
and more honorable
to have only one
relationship
at a time.

Question is
how long a time is decent?
and how soon after one may
the other follow
before the man
or the woman
is disreputed to be
easy?

And so what if he or she is?

More to the point -
interactions among
one's lovers would happen
in a small town
with only one blinking light
and be as unpredictable
in their effects
as in any city.

DAY DREAM OF YOU

I place my lips on your lips
warm cool portals through which
my tongue finds yours
as our bodies touch
even through our clothes
and our arms pull us together
the hard soft comfort of your embrace
the comfort of giving the same.

I lie with my thigh between yours
hot between yours
hot against your hot center
my eyes squaring yours
my lips on your lips
my tongue against your tongue
past unguarding teeth
fingers entwined
then loosed to wander
our touches soft hard
enough to cry
at the gifts we bring to bed.

I sit here and write these wishes
my lips untouched my tongue enclosed
my thigh feeling barren cloth
my chest wanting your chest
my back wanting your hands
my hands wanting you.

And you?
Who are you?
Today you are you, only you.
Some time ago I saw another.
Today I see you -
Tomorrow who?

The touch of love, like sleep and drink,
we need   we want   we need
not like food,
which gives only strength and satisfaction,
but like water, without which nothing,
like sleep, without which madness.

TO WOMEN IT MAY CONCERN

I age -
Growing softer.

What of it?

I have
Fingers
Lips
Tongue -

Am I less than
Would be
A lesbian lover?

No matter that I lack
The female gifts I seek...
Those are not
What draw you to me.

Let this penis
Take its time.

It comes with me,
Grateful for your touch,
A valued friend,
Attached, of course,
But not the essence
Anymore.

BEETHOVEN TRIO AT WINEMA BEACH

On a hard wood bench
in the day-drenched room by the sea
we sit intent on wordless songs
a deaf man heard and put on paper long ago.

A silent crowd surrounds us
most grey and lined
who have known tribulation
and sadness that come with age
while on the stage three young people
move to make his sounds.

The pianist's fingers tap a phrase –
a sequence of light pressures
I feel in my chest and on my skin –
arousing emotions then explained
by cries from rosined bows on strings
of cello and the violin.

Harmonies float like clouds distant over breaking waves.
Our shoulders touch and we allow our heat to flow.
Later, fingers pressing, we'll play our own adagio.

NEW VISION WITH OLD EYES

Hair grey or white and short
the stocky women
in laundered slacks
flannel shirts
and comfortable shoes
seem past sex
yet I know some
whose eyes flirt
as we talk of this and that
and I imagine how it would be
to lie naked with her
enjoying her skin
no longer concerned with
the making of new life
or betrayal of a spouse
no commitment other than
to be alive and feel what is
her hand gentle on my center
as mine rests on hers

SOUL MATE

Wanting you to see me as I see me
I compose myself in the mirror for you -
You see yourself.

EVENING FLIGHT

PROCRASTINATION

Surrounded by
disorder and dreck
bills to be paid
promises to be kept
things to be done
visions of what could be
should I the effort make,
I do nothing and inside ache
yearning for your touch.

Wanting and wanting
order and beauty
a stillness inside stays my hand
daring the gods
to punish me.

With nothing accomplished
I sit and write
allowing time
to closer bring
the fright that motivates.

EVENING FLIGHT

He looks east
to goose honks
from the river bank
beyond the dark trees.

The mostly clear sky
pale with sparse clouds
touched pink
by the setting sun
foretells a cold night.

The southerly breeze is gentle.

The geese are busy
beyond the dark trees
assembling squadrons for
their evening flight.

He is not busy.

He stands outside looking east
the open door a yellow patch
of light behind him
and his fears
loom black against the
coming moonless night.

The geese do not say
a storm is coming. So
perhaps it won't, tonight.
But it will someday.
Far away forces are
assembling their squadrons.

The breeze caresses
his temple tenderly,
as a butcher might ready
a bird for cutting.

His thoughts flutter.

He should
put up shutters, he should
tack down some shingles, he should
store provisions and firewood,
he should.

But he stands still.
Whatever can happen, will.

Black specks
above the dark trees
the geese
still talking
fly south
and are gone.

Quiet.

The sky's pinks have grayed.
The doorway brightens
as the dark trees hide.

He is alone.

He goes in the house
and closes the door.

POSSESSIONS

Piles of paper
piles of clothes
boxes full of what?
colonize all flat surfaces
and floors in the rooms of my house.

When life becomes clumsy
spaces between boxes too small to navigate
I rent a storage room or cubicle
and carry my possessions there.

Sorting is beyond me.

Unexamined
their destiny is
a dark space
like a refrigerator
lit by one bulb only when I look in -
vast contents, jumbled
boxes, piles
semiprecious rags, pictures,
papers, books, clothes, things,
piles and boxes –
retaining colors in the darkness
gaining odors and mold
and compressed shapes.

I have forgotten
or no longer know
without being still and
thinking for a long time
and not fully even then
what is in these rooms

in buildings of such rooms
behind padlocked doors
next to padlocked doors of
others who also live in excess.

Some rooms perhaps
belong to people in transit
from one home to another
to be emptied soon
not repositories like mine.

Each month I pay
to keep it all safe.

No more could I divest
myself of these ancient possessions
and remain myself
than a coffin could lose its remains
and remain an interment...

Or so it seems at the moment...

But who wants to live as a coffin?

MAKING PROGRESS

My daily path is narrow in this house
among accretions of years
I've not yet begun to cull
preferring to travel in the mind
or walk outdoors
while new mail and papers like dust
settle almost everywhere -
but only rarely now
do I buy or bring in things
(occasionally a book...)
that are not consumed
along the path
from bed to bath to kitchen
to the couch where I write
or eaten by the dog.

EMERGENCY

Silenced
by long inattention
the voice of self emerges
as procrastination.

What says the self?

No more!
Listen!
Unless I am caressed and fed,
held close and whispered to,
I will not move.
Nothing
can make me -
for I am a cloud
not to be tethered,
I am a stone
too smooth to grasp
too heavy to lift.
I could fly were I embraced,
invited to come into my own.
I know what will nourish us
and it is not this,
this thing you are about to bury us in.

DAILY RITUAL

SUNDAY MORNING

breezy street
leafy trees
morning sun
wine cool shade
walking the dog
to the café
thoughts of toast
and marmalade

GREYING

A fringe of grey
around his belly, on
his chin some white hairs...

These four years
he has grown mature -
from the dark-eyed soft pup
held in one hand jet black
to this tough dog
on the couch
beside me
snoring.

He seems satisfied with his life.

The mission he has accepted is to be.

There might be a decade more
(his kind lives fifteen years or so)
of his sound and weight
on my bed at night.

We grey together.

FIRST WALK AFTER

A deliciously chill wind
drives inland from the sea
beneath gray clouds.

Brown eyes agleam
the black dog
prances loose-leashed
beside me on the bridge.

I drink the cold air.

As my mind clears
a blue patch grows
in the sky.

No. The patch is imagined.
There is no blue out there.
Today truth is enough:

A delicious wind drizzles chill
droplets on my glasses and face
as my mind clears
and the black dog prances by my side.

DAILY RITUAL

putchie putchie
he said to the dog
who ignored the invitation
lying still

pitchki pitchki
the man offered
but the dog lay on
though one eye quivered

tchuki tchuki
pleaded the man
dangling the red leash -
the dog lay still
but for a slight tremor of tail

minchi pinchi
said the man
as he fixed the leash
to the harness -
the dog stood up easily
jumped off the couch
and moved to the door

good dog
said the man
and their walk began

THINKING OF TIME ON WINTER SOLSTICE

"I woke before dawn and thought it was early, but it wasn't..."   *said Carl Eagle Bell of Blaine, Oregon, on December 20th, 2009*

Somehow we have made all clocks agree
but for acknowledged measurable imperfections
and how far east or west we are of some line on the map.

Clocks can tell us if our appointed day
is to begin before or after dawn,
if an event is early or late.

Clock time is needed
to organize us,
say our taskmasters.

My dog knows when it's time for bed,
time for food, for going outside.
So what if these are just appetites,
the body's urgent needs?
Is that a bad way to mark time?
The dog never says, "I'm tired,
but it's not yet time for a nap."
I might command his wakefulness.
Putting on my coat or jingling some keys,
I might be his clock.
But for him, time is not a number.

RAIN

HOW TO EAT A D'ANJOU PEAR

Lift it gently from its litter.
Admire its pale green skin,
its sturdy curve.

Ask permission:
press a finger
against the swollen ring
around its stem.

You will know yes
if it yields just enough
to return your touch
as if you were pressing another
of your own fingertips.

Bathe it in clear water.

Cup its bottom in one hand.
With the other twist out the stem.

Kiss the smooth skin
around the hole.

Open your mouth.
Let your teeth sink in.

Look at the gleaming white flesh.
Let its sweetness fill you.

Eat all slowly
even the slippery black seeds.
Leave only that bristly little crown
at the blossom end.

Lick from your fingers
the last of the juice.

POCKETS

"Keep a poem in your pocket..."
           Beatrice Schenk de Regniers

My jeans today have five pockets.
In one only the thumb and forefinger fit
when a coin is needed. My shirt
has one over my left breast
sheltering a pen or two and the little camera
instead of cigarettes. My belt
carries a pouch for the cell phone.

Could I live naked even in warm tropics
with no pockets at hand? My daily companions
removed to a bag or knapsack or left behind?
Perhaps I'd leave home armed only with a poem?
a sonnet remembered, by Shakespeare perhaps,
or one I might make as I go? Yet
I'd miss the things and while
a knapsack's straps might hook the thumbs,
still remains the old question: Where to keep the hands
(when not tucked under crossed arms
or placed elbows out on the hips)?

Into the front pockets of my jeans –
as I stand at the open door
overlooking the town where I now live
feeling the cool air
seeing in the distance a triangle of ocean
beyond the river and the dunes -
I sometimes thrust both hands
thumbs out fingers in
tips approving thighs made hard
by walks with the dog and an occasional dance.

Sometimes each thumb comes in too
making the whole hand secure.

In one front pocket my fingers
graze a yellow knife
and keys - for house and car
for mailbox. In the other the soft handkerchief.

Of the two pockets behind
the right holds my wallet
with a little folding money if I'm lucky but
filled mostly with cards to tell
who I am
  what I can buy
    what I can drive
and scraps of history, receipts.

The left one is empty
almost all the time it seems.

I imagine a woman walking at my side
reaching four fingers in that pocket
her thumb hooked over its top
feeling my moving haunch
with companionable warmth.
Would there be room there for a poem?
Would it be a love poem?

WINTER ON THE OREGON COAST

Grey crags of surf
show through drizzle or rain
as you drive to acquire
some southern red grapes.

At Safeway, push open the car's door.
Venture a foot on the puddled asphalt.
Hold your hat's brim in the wind.
Rise slowly to stand without slipping.

Hope for dry socks,
for the balance you need
to avoid all depressions.

Buy an orange too at the market.
Heft its plump weight.
Smell the faraway summer.

SMASHED

He enters from the kitchen and
before he knows it, throws it.

The mug flies in a shallow arc
spinning slowly towards the large window
overlooking the town.
Brown liquid splatters.

Shards scatter over the wooden deck outside.
Cool sea air creeps into the room.

Ah… the window does not shatter.
The town sleeps peacefully beyond.

His arm remains calm at his side
the mug steady in hand.
He approaches the soft chair
by the window.

"Why am I so angry?"
he asks the dog and
pausing to consider the matter
sits to sip his tea.

TATA

(1895 – 1959)

I am astonished to see him sitting on the window ledge looking at me. He is slender with shiny black hair, younger than I am.

He is there in black and white. His cigarette disperses smoke into the quiet room air. One eye squints behind the smoke as he speaks softly. What is he saying? I can't hear. What is he thinking? Does he know all? Has he come to help me?

Did he manage life better than I? My father. My young father? Could I, in my white-haired age, offer him advice?

He is vivid on the window ledge. I am the ghost in the room. He is gone before I say anything. Before I even think to greet him.

He did right. He got us out of Europe, away from death in the madness of that war. For what? So I can sit here, alone, scribbling, on the hundred fifteenth anniversary of his birth, in a rainy town on the coast of Oregon? What other lives did he save? And his own? What of his own?

After I die, will my son someday see me too? In color? What would I try to tell him then?

THE PUBLIC LIBRARY

In our town
a building stands
filled with words
and music
of people from afar
from beyond the trees
beyond the seas
beyond the grave

Where one may read
and listen even
borrow for a while
such books
and records
as feed the mind
the eye
or please the ear

From this oasis
we take our fill
yet leave
the treasures
undiminished
so all may taste

Where to those who browse
(though they have books they own)
Knowledge
displays her ample charms
saying
  "Experience
   not Possession
   is your Wealth"

LOST MEMORIES

My family traveled light
on the journey from distant home
to uncertain future somewhere safe,
farther and farther from the cemeteries
and the people whose children
I can see in photographs
taken at birthday parties when I was three -
in festive clothes, sailor suits sometimes
and ceremonial hats, signaling a well-to-do existence
among pretty children,
whose names I no longer know.

Perhaps back then there were celebrations
of holidays other than birthdays
but the surrounding walls and furnishings,
the patterned rugs and throws,
are gone forever and so are the memories.

I was nine when the war from which we'd fled
was over. I don't remember whether
I remembered directly then
what I see in these photographs.
Were it not for the photo albums
considered precious enough for my parents
to take across continents and ocean
on trains, taxis, plane and ship,
and then brought by me to the bookshelf here,
the parents dead, I'd know even less.

Losing the rooms, the streets, the cemeteries,
I've lost memories too. I don't remember
celebrating any holidays when I was nine,
although recall my father sometimes
attending a synagogue on Yom Kippur.
I now know my parents were mourning.

A MOTHER'S LOVE

I turn the knob
To our mahagony front door.
Before I can push it,
The door opens before me.
She stands there,
Her eyes and mouth happy to see me.
The smile evaporates.
Her hand slaps me hard -
The only time I'd been slapped
In my young life.

"Where have you been?" she hisses,
"Don't you ever disappear like that again!"
Her blue eyes gleam.
I feel the sting on my right cheek.
Do tears come to my eyes?

She pulls me to her chest,
To her flowery scent.
"I was worried," she whispers.

RAIN

is more than we
can grab whole
relief from the parched
cold bone shiver in wind
splash of passionful delight
sweeping river of loss
tears to restore
tears of pain
quenching
drowning
renewal
on the horizon
a grey curtain
another act

ONLY ME

WIDOWER

I pretend to live here
among your things
in the house I sleep in
on one side of the bed

UNVEILING

we celebrate the life that has ended
the rabbi said
as we cried

celebrate by living

give in her memory
remember her song
her ways
her words
her loves
her gifts to each
remember
who you are because she lived

open your eyes
walk your own path
see
tell your story
share yourself with fellow travelers
listen
taste
touch
be open
allow yourself to be
touched

live

so those who eventually mourn you
may learn

A VOW

Pleasing woman
pleasing man
I've done more
more than I can.

Becoming empty
I bid adieu
suddenly fearless
becoming new.

Now I'm here
now I'll stay
I won't again
give me away.

MIXED METAPHORS

the past dies every day
compost from which grows
this moment -
new skin bare to the breeze

ONLY ME

All my me's will meet
one day
to kiss and dance
around my feet.

And then...

O then I'll be
O then I'll be
at last (what bliss!)
an only me
one day.

FREE MAN

Feet apart
on the ground
at ease
with space around,
a beckoning breeze
on my face.

Nevertheless...

I lack, I crave,
the knowing touch,
the soft embrace
of Woman.

CREDO OF THE MOMENT

Never again only one
But with each
Honest speech
Open skin
Caring
And
(Can it possibly be?)
Excitement and joy

TOSSING WORDS

Tossing a salad improves it.

Tossing most anything
improves the void left behind.

Tossing words

... back and forth
... out the window
... turning a phrase
... watching them fly
... catching the meaning

improves the tosser.

Tossing back and forth ties.

Tossing out the window clears the air.

Turning a phrase exposes its conceit.

Watching words fly is seeing
with the third eye.

Catching a meaning is a joy
though sorrow be its name.

UNLEASHED

ANTICIPATION

1. Conquered

Clicking chopsticks
over our sushi
her delicate teeth
framed by red lips
her simple words
our eyes connecting
I yearn to touch her
to drink in all ways
the calm
another dimension
to the whirling woman
I met a month ago
her teeth on my shoulder
a love bite I thought
surprised on the dance floor.

2. Do I Dare Disturb?

Six days of work
nights in a shared flat
Sunday visits to her mother -
life regular and full
many years now.

This she told when we met
for sushi and tempura.

"My hand," she said, "is there
when my body feels a need." Yet
she took my arm as we walked
to the parking lot and
by her car she took my kiss
first on the corner of her mouth
then the second softly briefly
lips on lips.

3. Dinner Date

I hold her elbow
and guide her to our table.

We talk while we share
a dish of salmon and small
red potatoes with parsley
and sip red wine.

I imagine as we talk,
warmth and scent
from her slender form.

Will we embrace in the night?
Will our skins touch, here hot
here cool, here smooth
here hair?   Continuing
our conversation?

How does that happen?
Crossing the invisible
barrier between public face
and private body?

We look at each other's mouths,
and talk on, circling
in a dance
of thought and yearning.

There are no prescribed steps
as we collaborate
to make what might
or might not be.

4. A Kiss

From your lips to mine
a small first kiss
light as a child's
brief as one chirp
yet enough
to feed the many mouths
of my roaring lust.

5. Your Hand

Your hand says to my hand
Let's play.

Your hand that has touched yourself
touches my hand.

Will it teach mine to touch you?

6. Anticipation

He takes her hand over the table.
It is small and shaped like his
warm damp and tentative
but she does not withdraw it
and they talk of becoming lovers.
.
I'd like to, but I'm not sure I'm ready, she says.

Her days are so full.
When she returns from visiting her mother
she may just spend Sunday afternoon napping.
We can do that together, he says.
She smiles and says
we should talk on Sunday.

He spends Saturday cleaning his apartment.

YEARS HAVE PASSED

Seems decades since we lay together
in sunlight filtered by venetian blinds
our zebra skins a contour map of love.

Now you lie in another room
your head perhaps on another chest
as here I caress another breast.

No, I think of you but now and then
as when the light is right
and then I wonder
do you think of me?

UNLEASHED

1. Unleashed

Unleashed
Reborn
Clamoring for expression
Are the spirit
The passions
Appetites
Long submerged!
Long thought dead!

How did this happen?

Rain brought us together
Imagined crash of thunder
In imagined heavy electric air
Started a conversation without end
Fertilized by pleasure
Of finding a friend

Unleashed and frolicking
Are the spirit
The passions
Appetites
Now giving rebirth
To us both.

2. Très Intime

You've given me a key
to your secret room
where we swim in tears
holding hands
abandoning fears
laughing
touching
talking
très intime,
the walls around
not between.

3. jj comings

i like the poem
you just sent me
just as yesterday
you sent me
where i hope
you'll soon join me
where soon we'll
send we
again

4. Don't Stop

Envelop me
in your lush
jungle of love
O lusty
puma!

Our ways wend
parallel
magical
entwined.

Your hot heart
your cool tongue
your deep eyes
your smooth lips
are my companions
on this voyage...

Don't stop!

A SHORT AFFAIR

1. Amazed

She walks
across the room
her hair loose
her naked body
glowing in the lamplight
her slender nude body
walking in comfort
before my eyes.

She has emerged
tall slender unbowed
from the chrysalis
of clothes
and diffidence

and I am in awe
of her white golden beauty
her gentle power
enchanted by her beauty
in awe of her graceful
and calm walk to our bed
amazed by her delight to be
with me.

2. Winter Fantasy

Bell-like clangs from
the black iron stove
and the hiss of wet logs
give the rhythm to which
we dance naked together
on the wool rug
as our dogs watch.

3. Shining Fruit

Our garden bore berries last year
squash tomatoes beans
although the carrot crop was poor.

Our hands chopped
onions and garlic
ginger
for dishes new to us
spiced turmeric cumin coriander
comforted with
couscous brown rice brown pasta.

Our nights were warm
bodies touching
the wood stove crackling
a dog's weight on the blankets
anchoring us
as we talked loved and slept.

We might have lived
forever this way
but our minds
first enchanted
by intelligence and art
now argued
their tired cases and insisted
on more or less -
dredging from our pasts
poisons concealed
by the shining fruits we'd enjoyed.

There were no fruit in winter.

Spring is coming.
I'm frightened.

4. Our Ship Sinks

Out of view of any shore
my life raft floats becalmed
not far from yours
beneath a clouded sky.

Your angry voice accuses me
of being the travel agent
who to both of us had lied.

The ship sinks before our gaze.

Now we must decide.

Shall we to each other cling
or make our ways alone?

5. A Short Affair

We met on the road
and you took my hand.
We were going the same way.

"Let's run, " you cried,
"Let's run to the end together!"
But I hung back,
"Why hurry?
I have much to carry.
Let's walk together slowly..."

"If you don't throw
your past away,
you don't love me enough,"
you cried, "I want to be
going somewhere. Come!"

As I thought and thought
your hand slipped out of mine.

I heard your faint "Good bye."

IN THE CLEAR

SECOND ADOLESCENCE

This time
like the first
mixes childhood
and maturity.

The direction may differ -
but the cauldron seethes
and experiments are afoot.

Again the task is to become.

This time, to build him
who soon will be saying good-bye -
on his way to the second nursery
or on his way out that door.

BEING STILL

The child felt pain at nothing to do.
The growing man smoked to busy himself.

At his prime, ambition's willing tool,
he fretted when not pursuing wealth.

Time today is a green-blue pool.
Mysteries flicker in its depths.

The lengthening past invites review.
Boredom was an affliction of youth.

IN THE CLEAR

My parents, my wife, all dead.
Children grown, able
to care for their children.

Pensions let me
live well enough
my health is good enough
to let me dance
and talk with others
over a glass of wine -
to let me work
now and then.

All seems possible
in this moment of joy
this moment of peace
this moment of trembling
with tears of sadness -
in this moment of power.

What to do with this wealth?

LOOKING OLD

The tavern's door burst open as I approached.
A chunky gray-haired man hesitated.

"Age before beauty..." he offered.
"Hmm," I said, "Hard to tell..."
We faced each other.

He stepped through, then turned,
"I'm sixty. For sure I'm younger than you."

GETTING OLD

Now the plump curve
pleasing to the gaze
is an invitation no longer -
I've been dropped from the list.

NOT QUITE OVER, YET...

A late quartet by Haydn,
Then one of Schubert's...

Dates in the program show
Papa Haydn was my age when he died.

Schubert only thirty-one at his end
made some 800 pieces in sixteen years.

Sixteen may exceed what I have left,
but there is this poem, and
maybe one tomorrow.

THE WEIGHT OF WELLBEING

sagging
in the mirror
above this desk
his wattles displease him

he frowns

remembers carrying a smile
now too heavy

the search for meaning
has exhausted him

no longer does he easily recall
the trivia of recent days

is the mind departing
too heavy too?

he yawns

he compresses his lips
in concentration
and looks at himself

without intention
the corners of that mouth lift
making the face familiar

heavy to carry
but worth it
the substitution of burdens

I WANT

because I seem to please

> *taking in – sending out*
> *extending myself*
> *into or around*

you

> *is this about writing?*
> *or making love?*
> *or cooking together*
> *and eating -*
> *little lip smacks and smiles?*

to touch and be touched

WAKING UP

"I saw the best minds of my generation destroyed ..."
Allen Ginsberg, *Howl*

When, goaded by loss, I rise
from my sleep of youth
and moneyed middle age,
and open my eyes to see through
the misted illusions I've lived,
rage clears the way to begin
to become what could have been sooner,
had I avoided what so many
of the best minds of my generation
were destroyed by – comfort.

ALMOST A SONNET

when the breeze leafs by me
my weight steady on two legs apart
feet flat on the ground
when the drizzle drops refresh
my face, my thighs hard,
knees slightly bent, ready for all
and no one says no! don't! or stop!
I feel the power of blood tough in my veins
splendid under my skin
and someone says hello how are you,
I grow taller and invincible
in my deluded mind
for the moment happy
and it doesn't matter for what.

JUST AS

AS TIME PASSES

as time passes
there is less reason to do
what need not outlive me
less need to please
those who will not mourn
less fear of being thought
a fool or other failure
and more drive to say
what it all has meant.

STILL CLIMBING

I entered my eighth decade a widower
having been married for forty-five of my fifty adult years.

A rolling stone gathers none
but its downhill journey is short.
Yet whose is not?

Death's visit and her departure taught me
life ends too soon.

Statistics say the longer you stay alive
the longer you will live.

She left me her dog.
At the time, his life expectancy
was fifteen years, like mine.

Dogs and men age at different speeds.
Statistics now say I am likely to mourn him.

What am I saying? with poetic license?
I don't have those statistics on hand.

I want to live
not as a stone of any sort.
I want to walk not roll – climb maybe;
to talk; to work and to love;
to gather and discard.
I want to be aware.

And to give.
Do I have anything to give?
Left to give?
Easy to say I have only my needs to offer.
Yet, I've said such.

But one life to give, is all.
But not quite willing to give it all
yet.

To give pleasure
To give comfort
To give knowledge
To give sustenance
To give friendship
To be seen and felt

To let another see how she or he affects me
To make something
To write
To show
To read aloud
To dance

A simple life,
Despite awareness

Awareness of death and pain -
Of my grandmother being killed
by soldiers.
Of another grandmother, an aunt, and a cousin
also killed for no reason but their heritage.

Of cruelty.
Of my mother aging demented
dying tied to a hospital bed.
Of the lust for life
being a destroyer of life -
Young men in musth.

Oh, God, if you exist
explain yourself.

Silence from above.

Why above?
Perhaps God permeates the soil
residing in magma and shit,
a miasma penetrating all. Why
would He/She/It care about us?
We, a plague upon the planet, soon
to be a plague upon space too? Our
cities and mines like skin cancers on the face
of our Earth? Our effusions a poison to other
life, even our own? Are we worthy of care?

If God did not care, we would not have God.
Create your God as You would Be.
Each of us a universe, in our minds all.

When I die, will all go?

AN HONEST MAN

except when speaking
                white or black lies

except when being
                polite or spiteful

except when seeking
                to spare or to hurt

except when avoiding
                pain or humiliation

except when not

KINDNESS OF STRANGERS

Those
who learn my faults
and see my lapses,
unadorned by memory
of my announced self,
expect nothing else
than they see.

They
can be kind,
and I'm learning
to not tell them
who I'd rather be.

OUT OF GAS

Today again the choice
to rest
or to go on
for the next twenty years
or days ...
to rest and dry into dust
or to rest and grow again
from remnants and the air
because
what brought us here
by way of many cities and villages
in which we've left traces
and children...
is out of gas
the journey exciting but in the past
and we must find another way to go
another way to be
or not

STRATEGY

In a crowd
unlikely to be singled out
yet vulnerable to
mass movements or epidemic
we are not safe.

Standing alone
exposed on all sides
not safe either.

As I cling to you
have I shared the danger
or have I doubled my exposure?

At least we warm each other.

ACCOUNTING FOR AMBITION
(STEERING FOR SUCCESS)

"... yer puts on yer pants one leg at a time, don't ya?"

We often are paid
in the common coin of common man
with a slap on the back, a snort and a sneer.

The body's overhead is ever there -
fine tuning makes all the difference.
Tilting tip feathers steer the drifting gull.
Trims of sail and rudder propel the boat into the wind.

This business of living well or large is no yacht race.
Along my passage to oblivion, I want
to reach the soft success of do no harm
to honor both
       shit and wisdom
       piss and art
       orgasm and love
       appetite and compassion
with a laugh besides
on both sides of each coin.

THERE OUGHT TO BE A LAW

he is dead
his last thought an
equilibrating blip
of wetware's electric chemistry

there will be no trace
of its architecture
its graceful enunciation
of a subtle truth

(a multi-hued sunset
over deserted dunes
seen only by unspeaking lizards
and snakes)

too bad the universe's rules
don't conserve unexpressed ideas -
only eternal matter and energy
uncommunicating atoms and ergs

A SOURCE?

If pain is a warning,
a call to change,
to what end constant pain -
unremitting, yielding not to recoil
or change in position
or stretch
or pills?

What purpose has such pain?
Such as requires unconsciousness
to relieve, or, at least, attenuation
of awareness to permit sleep?

Whether purpose is implied, or not, is moot.
I want there to be an intention, someone's.
With purpose would come hope of change.

Does one ever get used to it?
get to not feeling it?
Constant pain, like eternal damnation,
seems an error, incompetence on the part of
the Creator, the Manager, or the Mistress.
Or is it a pin placed
in the voodoo doll?

Only engagement of the mind
seems to help reliably,
but getting engaged is not easy
in the presence of pain.

Writing about it,
though I'd have thought
focus would maintain it,
makes pain abate...

Is this a source of art?

JUST AS

just as I see clearly
and feel in the clear
a pensioner
with few obligations
to others
just as all things seem possible
the fears of youth gone
the courage of survival present
the unused talents
emerging from their burial
in the muck of worldly ambition

just as I see others clearly
and can talk and laugh
and make love with joy
without care
just as all seems possible
for the first time
and excitement builds
to write
to paint
to live and tell my story
to leave marks on the minds and eyes
of others

just so comes death
peeping around the trees
that line this road
through which I glimpse the setting sun...

and I have to be on guard
against rushing to make complete
the hopes unfilled
because hurry would destroy
the very substance from which could grow
a self I could love
as I say good bye.

NOTES

The quotation (page vi) is from an interview of Petersen conducted by Drew Myron on 10 Oct 2011.

WHEN I WRITE (page 4) was drafted during a workshop taught by Joan Dobbie at a NW Poets' Concord; she offered each of us a fresh fruit (mine was a tangerine) and asked us to go outside and contemplate our surroundings at the coast in Newport, Oregon, for about 15 minutes before returning to write a poem.

In MEMORIES AT STARBUCKS IN HOLLYWOOD (pages 59-62) and in I WALK THE STREETS, OPEN (page 69) most names and initials are fictionalized.

In WALK DOWN VINE STREET (page 67), AA means Alcoholics Anonymous.

"Tata" is one way of saying "Dad" in Polish, the language of my parents' household. (TATA, page 114)

HOW TO EAT A D'ANJOU PEAR (page 109) was launched off a "springboard" at one of Paulann Petersen's workshops. I no longer recall the specific prompt.

LOST MEMORIES (page 116) was written in response to Paulann Petersen's challenge, at another of her poetry workshops, to write about memories from a favorite holiday celebrated at a specific childhood age.

WAKING UP (page 149) was inspired at a special open mic in Manzanita, Oregon; the organizers, Kathie Hightower and Vera Wildauer, supplied several one-line quotes from famous poets and asked each of us to choose one quote to use as a prompt for, or as part of, a poem to be written within 10 minutes right then and there.

AUTOBIOGRAPHICAL NOTE
(Julius Jortner, 2014)

I was born in 1936 in Cernăuți, a town in Romania near the border with Poland. Borders have shifted over the decades; Cernăuți now is Chernivtsi in Ukraine. My parents were Polish nationals with a business in Romania. They contrived to leave in late1940, heading south and out of Europe to escape the war and the Holocaust. Their mothers, sisters, and some nieces remained in Poland and most did not survive. We found refuge in Bombay, India, where I learned English. In 1946, after World War II ended, we came to the USA, where I've lived since, first in New York City, then in Los Angeles, and now, for the last 20 years or so, in Pacific City, Oregon.

My schooling includes a diploma from Stuyvesant High School and a Bachelor of Mechanical Engineering from the Cooper Union for the Advancement of Science and Art, both in New York City, and a Master of Engineering from the University of California in Los Angeles.

I've experienced marriages, fatherhood, divorce, love, friendship, widowerhood, and work (as a research engineer and as a freelance photojournalist), among other aspects of a mostly peaceful life.

A few of my poems have appeared in *Four and Twenty*, an online journal of short-form poetry, in publications of the Northwest Poets' Concord, and in *North Coast Squid* (in which some of my photos also appear). You may hear me read on the Web at *oregonpoeticvoices.org*.

This is my first book of poems.

ACKNOWLEDGEMENTS

Among those who encouraged me to continue to write poems and to read poems aloud here and there were David Bellomy, Sonya Beebe, David Bicknell, Marilyn Burkhardt, Travis Champ, Terry Frost, John Fiedler, Naomi Gladstone Grady, Steve Herndon, Marshall Jackson, Sue Jenkins, Matt Love, Melissa Madenski, Sandra Mason, Susan Friedman Milch, Catherine Rickbone, Roger Ritchey, Diane Robinson, Fran Saslow, Barbara Schuetze, Diana Sears, and David Starr. I hope only a few are disappointed in the results as presented in this book. I apologize to those whose names I've omitted. I thank them all.

I thank the Monday Writers of the upper Oregon coast, the Tuesday Writers of Waldport, and the organizers and attendees of the monthly open-mic events at Lincoln City's Driftwood library. These informal groups of interested and interesting writers gave me valuable attention and comments. Also important to me were opportunities to read poems at open mics in Newport, hosted by Writers on the Edge, and in Manzanita, hosted by the Manzanita Writers Series.

I thank PLAYA at Summer Lake, Oregon, for granting me in September 2014 the residency that provided solitude and time to work out the plan for this book.

I thank Shirley Denise Brown for her life-giving attention and encouragement during the months I was compiling this book.

I am deeply grateful for the three decades I was given to be with Carolee June Robbins, for (among other gifts) her insights and her creative spirit some of which I like to think rubbed off on me.

I acknowledge and thank the editors of the following print publications and online magazines in which some versions of these poems have appeared or been accepted for publication:

Tuesday: The Laurel Tree, There Ought To Be A Law, Refugees, What It Means

Concord: Second Adolescence, What It Means

North Coast Squid: Evening Flight, How To Eat A D'Anjou Pear, Taught by Salt.

4and20poetry.com: Remnants, At The Seashore (the middle stanza of Black and Blue), Soul Mate, Winter Morning Over The City, Widower. Alas, *4and20poetry* ceased operations in Nov 2014.

oregonpoeticvoices.com: Second Adolescence, Mixed Metaphors, Heading Home In Winter, Late Ambitions.

Made in the USA
Charleston, SC
06 March 2015